An answer to some papers lately printed, concerning the authority of the Catholick Church in matters of faith and the reformation of the Church of England. (1686)

Edward Stillingfleet

An answer to some papers lately printed, concerning the authority of the Catholick Church in matters of faith and the reformation of the Church of England.

Stillingfleet, Edward, 1635-1699.

Errata: p. 24

[1], 24 p.

Dublin : Reprinted by Jos. Ray for Rob. Thornton, 1686.

Wing / S5563

English

Reproduction of the original in the Union Theological Seminary (New York, N. Y.) Library

Early English Books Online (EEBO) Editions

Imagine holding history in your hands.

Now you can. Digitally preserved and previously accessible only through libraries as Early English Books Online, this rare material is now available in single print editions. Thousands of books written between 1475 and 1700 and ranging from religion to astronomy, medicine to music, can be delivered to your doorstep in individual volumes of high-quality historical reproductions.

We have been compiling these historic treasures for more than 70 years. Long before such a thing as "digital" even existed, ProQuest founder Eugene Power began the noble task of preserving the British Museum's collection on microfilm. He then sought out other rare and endangered titles, providing unparalleled access to these works and collaborating with the world's top academic institutions to make them widely available for the first time. This project furthers that original vision.

These texts have now made the full journey -- from their original printing-press versions available only in rare-book rooms to online library access to new single volumes made possible by the partnership between artifact preservation and modern printing technology. A portion of the proceeds from every book sold supports the libraries and institutions that made this collection possible, and that still work to preserve these invaluable treasures passed down through time.

This is history, traveling through time since the dawn of printing to your own personal library.

Initial Proquest EEBO Print Editions collections include:

Early Literature

This comprehensive collection begins with the famous Elizabethan Era that saw such literary giants as Chaucer, Shakespeare and Marlowe, as well as the introduction of the sonnet. Traveling through Jacobean and Restoration literature, the highlight of this series is the Pollard and Redgrave 1475-1640 selection of the rarest works from the English Renaissance.

Early Documents of World History

This collection combines early English perspectives on world history with documentation of Parliament records, royal decrees and military documents that reveal the delicate balance of Church and State in early English government. For social historians, almanacs and calendars offer insight into daily life of common citizens. This exhaustively complete series presents a thorough picture of history through the English Civil War.

Historical Almanacs

Historically, almanacs served a variety of purposes from the more practical, such as planting and harvesting crops and plotting nautical routes, to predicting the future through the movements of the stars. This collection provides a wide range of consecutive years of "almanacks" and calendars that depict a vast array of everyday life as it was several hundred years ago.

Early History of Astronomy & Space

Humankind has studied the skies for centuries, seeking to find our place in the universe. Some of the most important discoveries in the field of astronomy were made in these texts recorded by ancient stargazers, but almost as impactful were the perspectives of those who considered their discoveries to be heresy. Any independent astronomer will find this an invaluable collection of titles arguing the truth of the cosmic system.

Early History of Industry & Science

Acting as a kind of historical Wall Street, this collection of industry manuals and records explores the thriving industries of construction; textile, especially wool and linen; salt; livestock; and many more.

Early English Wit, Poetry & Satire

The power of literary device was never more in its prime than during this period of history, where a wide array of political and religious satire mocked the status quo and poetry called humankind to transcend the rigors of daily life through love, God or principle. This series comments on historical patterns of the human condition that are still visible today.

Early English Drama & Theatre

This collection needs no introduction, combining the works of some of the greatest canonical writers of all time, including many plays composed for royalty such as Queen Elizabeth I and King Edward VI. In addition, this series includes history and criticism of drama, as well as examinations of technique.

Early History of Travel & Geography

Offering a fascinating view into the perception of the world during the sixteenth and seventeenth centuries, this collection includes accounts of Columbus's discovery of the Americas and encompasses most of the Age of Discovery, during which Europeans and their descendants intensively explored and mapped the world. This series is a wealth of information from some the most groundbreaking explorers.

Early Fables & Fairy Tales

This series includes many translations, some illustrated, of some of the most well-known mythologies of today, including Aesop's Fables and English fairy tales, as well as many Greek, Latin and even Oriental parables and criticism and interpretation on the subject.

Early Documents of Language & Linguistics

The evolution of English and foreign languages is documented in these original texts studying and recording early philology from the study of a variety of languages including Greek, Latin and Chinese, as well as multilingual volumes, to current slang and obscure words. Translations from Latin, Hebrew and Aramaic, grammar treatises and even dictionaries and guides to translation make this collection rich in cultures from around the world.

Early History of the Law

With extensive collections of land tenure and business law "forms" in Great Britain, this is a comprehensive resource for all kinds of early English legal precedents from feudal to constitutional law, Jewish and Jesuit law, laws about public finance to food supply and forestry, and even "immoral conditions." An abundance of law dictionaries, philosophy and history and criticism completes this series.

Early History of Kings, Queens and Royalty

This collection includes debates on the divine right of kings, royal statutes and proclamations, and political ballads and songs as related to a number of English kings and queens, with notable concentrations on foreign rulers King Louis IX and King Louis XIV of France, and King Philip II of Spain. Writings on ancient rulers and royal tradition focus on Scottish and Roman kings, Cleopatra and the Biblical kings Nebuchadnezzar and Solomon.

Early History of Love, Marriage & Sex

Human relationships intrigued and baffled thinkers and writers well before the postmodern age of psychology and self-help. Now readers can access the insights and intricacies of Anglo-Saxon interactions in sex and love, marriage and politics, and the truth that lies somewhere in between action and thought.

Early History of Medicine, Health & Disease

This series includes fascinating studies on the human brain from as early as the 16th century, as well as early studies on the physiological effects of tobacco use. Anatomy texts, medical treatises and wound treatment are also discussed, revealing the exponential development of medical theory and practice over more than two hundred years.

Early History of Logic, Science and Math

The "hard sciences" developed exponentially during the 16th and 17th centuries, both relying upon centuries of tradition and adding to the foundation of modern application, as is evidenced by this extensive collection. This is a rich collection of practical mathematics as applied to business, carpentry and geography as well as explorations of mathematical instruments and arithmetic; logic and logicians such as Aristotle and Socrates; and a number of scientific disciplines from natural history to physics.

Early History of Military, War and Weaponry

Any professional or amateur student of war will thrill at the untold riches in this collection of war theory and practice in the early Western World. The Age of Discovery and Enlightenment was also a time of great political and religious unrest, revealed in accounts of conflicts such as the Wars of the Roses.

Early History of Food

This collection combines the commercial aspects of food handling, preservation and supply to the more specific aspects of canning and preserving, meat carving, brewing beer and even candy-making with fruits and flowers, with a large resource of cookery and recipe books. Not to be forgotten is a "the great eater of Kent," a study in food habits.

Early History of Religion

From the beginning of recorded history we have looked to the heavens for inspiration and guidance. In these early religious documents, sermons, and pamphlets, we see the spiritual impact on the lives of both royalty and the commoner. We also get insights into a clergy that was growing ever more powerful as a political force. This is one of the world's largest collections of religious works of this type, revealing much about our interpretation of the modern church and spirituality.

Early Social Customs

Social customs, human interaction and leisure are the driving force of any culture. These unique and quirky works give us a glimpse of interesting aspects of day-to-day life as it existed in an earlier time. With books on games, sports, traditions, festivals, and hobbies it is one of the most fascinating collections in the series.

The BiblioLife Network

This project was made possible in part by the BiblioLife Network (BLN), a project aimed at addressing some of the huge challenges facing book preservationists around the world. The BLN includes libraries, library networks, archives, subject matter experts, online communities and library service providers. We believe every book ever published should be available as a high-quality print reproduction; printed on-demand anywhere in the world. This insures the ongoing accessibility of the content and helps generate sustainable revenue for the libraries and organizations that work to preserve these important materials.

The following book is in the "public domain" and represents an authentic reproduction of the text as printed by the original publisher. While we have attempted to accurately maintain the integrity of the original work, there are sometimes problems with the original work or the micro-film from which the books were digitized. This can result in minor errors in reproduction. Possible imperfections include missing and blurred pages, poor pictures, markings and other reproduction issues beyond our control. Because this work is culturally important, we have made it available as part of our commitment to protecting, preserving, and promoting the world's literature.

GUIDE TO FOLD-OUTS MAPS and OVERSIZED IMAGES

The book you are reading was digitized from microfilm captured over the past thirty to forty years. Years after the creation of the original microfilm, the book was converted to digital files and made available in an online database.

In an online database, page images do not need to conform to the size restrictions found in a printed book. When converting these images back into a printed bound book, the page sizes are standardized in ways that maintain the detail of the original. For large images, such as fold-out maps, the original page image is split into two or more pages

Guidelines used to determine how to split the page image follows:

• Some images are split vertically; large images require vertical and horizontal splits.
• For horizontal splits, the content is split left to right.
• For vertical splits, the content is split from top to bottom.
• For both vertical and horizontal splits, the image is processed from top left to bottom right.

AN
ANSWER
TO SOME
PAPERS

Lately Printed, concerning the

AUTHORITY

OF THE

CATHOLICK CHURCH

In MATTERS of FAITH, and the
REFORMATION of the
CHURCH of ENGLAND.

[Edward Stillingfleet]

DUBLIN,

Reprinted by *Jof. Ray,* on *Colledge Green,* for *Rob Thornton,*
at the Leather-Bottle in *Skinner Row.* MDCLXXXVI.

AN
ADVERTISEMENT.

IF the Papers here answered, had not been so publickly dispersed through the Nation, a due Respect to the Name they bear, would have kept the Author from publishing any Answer to them. But because they may now fall into many hands, who without some assistance may not readily resolve some difficulties started by them, He thought it not unbecoming his duty to God and the King, to give a clearer light to the Things contained in them. And it can be no reflection on the Authority of a Prince, for a private Subject to examine a piece of Coyn as to its just value, though it bears His Image and Superscription upon it. In matters that concern Faith and Salvation, we must prove all things, and hold fast that which is good.

AN

AN
ANSWER
TO THE
FIRST PAPER.

IF all men could *believe as they pleased*, I should not have fail'd of satisfaction in this *First Paper*, the Design of it being to put an end *to Particular Disputes*, to which I am so little a Friend, that I could have been glad to have found, as much reason in it to convince, as I saw there was a fair appearance to deceive. But there is a *Law in our Minds* distinct from that of our *Inclinations* ; and out of a just and due regard to That, we must examine the most plausible Writings, thô back'd with the greatest Authority, before we yield our Assent unto them.

If particular Controversies about *Matters of Faith* could be ended by a Principle, *as visible as that the Scripture is in Print*, all men of sence would soon give over Disputing ; for none who dare believe what they see, can call that in Question. But what if *the Church*, whose *Authority*, it is said, *they must submit to*, will not allow them to believe what they see ? How then can this be a sufficient reason to perswade them to believe the Church, *because it is as visible as that the Scripture is in Print ?* Unless we must only use our senses to find out the Church, and renounce them assoon as we have done it. Which is a very bad requital of them, and no great Honour to the Church which requires it.

But with all due submission, it is no more *visible that the Roman Church is the Catholick Church*, than it is, *that a part is the whole*, and the most corrupt part, *that one Church, which Christ hath here upon Earth*.

It is agreed among all Christians, *That Christ can have but one Church upon Earth, as there is but one Lord, one Faith, one Baptism.* And this is that Church *we profess to believe in the two Creeds.* But if those, *who made those Creeds for our direction,* had intended the Roman Catholick Church, why was it not so expressed? How came it to pass that such a limitation of the sense of Christs Catholick Church to the Roman, should never be put to Persons to be Baptized in any Age of the Church? For I do not find in the Office of Baptism, even in the Roman Church, that it is required that they believe the Roman Catholick Church, or that they deny the validity of Baptism out of the Communion of the Roman Church. From whence it is to me as *visible as that the Scripture is in Print,* that the Church of Rome it self doth not believe that it is, *the one Catholick Church mentioned in the two Creeds.* For then it must void all Baptism out of its Communion, which it hath never yet done: And as long as Baptism doth enter Persons into the Catholick Church, it is impossible, that all who have the true form of Baptism, though out of the Communion of the Roman Church, should be Members of the Catholick Church, and yet the Communion of the Roman and Catholick be all one; as it must be if the Roman Church, be the Catholick and Apostolick Church professed in the Creeds.

If we had been so happy to have lived in those Blessed Times, *when the multitude of them that believed were of one heart, and of one soul,* it had been no difficulty to have shewed that *one visible Church, which Christ had here upon Earth.* But they must be great strangers to the History of the Church, who have not heard of the early and great Divisions in the Communion of it. And there was a remarkable difference in the Nature of those Schisms, which happened in the Church; which being not considered hath been the occasion of great misapplication of the sayings of the Ancients about the *One Catholick Church.* Some did so break off Communion with other parts of the Catholick Church, as to challenge that Title wholly to themselves; as was evident in the case of the Novatians and Donatists; for they rebaptiz'd all that embraced their Communion. Others were cast out of Communion upon particular differences; which were not supposed to be of such a nature, as to make them no members of the Catholick Church. So the Bishops of Rome excommunicated the Bishops of Asia for not keeping Easter when They did; and the Bishops both of Asia and Africa, for not allowing the Baptism of Hereticks. But is it reasonable to suppose, that upon these Differences they shut out all those Holy Bishops and Martyrs from the possibility of Salvation, by excluding them from their Communion? If not, then there may be different Communions among Christians, which may still continue *Part* of the Catholick Church; and consequently no one Member of such a Division ought to
assume

affume to it felf the *Title* and *Authority* of the *One Catholick Church.* But if any *One Part* doth fo, though never fo great and confpicuous, it is guilty of the fame Prefumption with the *Novatians* and *Donatifts,* and is as much caufe of the Schifms, which happen thereupon in the Church, as they were.

For a long time before the Reformation, there had been great and confiderable breaches, between the *Eaftern* and *Weftern Churches;* infomuch that they did renounce each others Communion. And in thefe Differences four *Patriarchal Churches* joined together againft the fifth, *viz.* that of the B fhop of *Rome.* But the Eaftern Patriarchs finking in their Power, by the horrible Invafion of the Enemies of the Chriftian Faith; and the Bifhops of *Rome* advancing themfelves to fo much Authority, by the advantages they took from the kindnefs of fome Princes, and the *Weaknefs* of others, They would hear of no other terms of accommodation with the Eaftern Churches, but by an intire fubmiffion to the *Pope as Head of the Catholick Church.* Which all the Churches of the Eaft refufed, however different among themfelves; and to this day look on the Pope's Supremacy as an Innovation in the Church, and Ufurpation on the Rights of the other Patriarchs and B fhops. In all thofe Churches the *Two Creeds are profeffed,* true Baptifm adminiftred, and an undoubted Succeffion of Bifhops from the Apoftles; How then come They to be excluded from being *Parts* of the *One Catholick and Apoftolick Church?* And if they be not excluded, how can the *Roman Church* affume to it felf that glorious Title: So that it feems to me *as vifible as that the Scripture is in Print,* that the *Roman Church* neither is, nor can be that *One Church,* which Chrift left upon Earth.

And this Principle being removed (which ought to be taken for granted; fince it can never be proved) we muft unavoidably *enter into the Ocean of Particular Difputes.* And I know no reafon any can have to be fo afraid of it, fince we have fo fure a Compafs, as the Holy Scripture to direct our paffage. But the reafon of avoiding *particular Difputes is,* becaufe the evidence is too clear in them, that the *Church of Rome* hath notorioufly deviated from this infallible Rule. And it is as impoffible for a Church, which hath erred, to be Infallible, as for a Church really Infallible, to err. But if a Church pretend to prove her Infallibility by Texts, which are not fo clear, as thofe which prove her to have actually erred; then we have greater reafon to recede from her Errors, than to be deceived with fuch a fallible pretence to Infallibility.

Well !

Well! *But it is not left to every phantastical mans head to believe as he pleases, but to the Church.*

And is it indeed left to the Church *to believe as it pleases?* But the meaning I suppose is, that those, who reject the Authority of the Roman Catholick Church, do leave every man to believe according to his own fancy. Certainly those of the *Church of England,* cannot be liable to any imputation of this Nature. For *our Church* receives the three Creeds, and embraces the four General Councils, and professes to hold nothing contrary to any Universal Tradition of the Church from the Apostles times. And we have often offered to put the Controversies between *Us,* and the *Church* of *Rome* upon that issue. And do not those rather *believe as they please,* who believe the *Roman Church* to be the *Catholick Church,* without any colour from Scriptures, Antiquity or Reason? Do not *those believe as they please,* who can believe against the most convincing evidence of their own senses? Do not *those believe as they please,* who can reconcile the lawfulness of the Worship of Images, with Gods forbidding it, the Communion in one kind, with Chrifts Institution, and the praying in an unknown Tongue with the 14 *Ch.* of the first Epistle to the *Corinthians?*

But all these and many other Abfurdities may go down by vertue of the Churches Authority, *to whom,* it is said, *Chrift left the Power upon Earth to govern us in matters of Faith.* We do not deny that the Church hath Authority of declaring matters of Faith, or else it never could have condemn'd the Antient Herefies. But then we must consider the difference between the *Universal Church* in a General and free Council, declaring the sense of Scripture in Articles of Faith, generally received in the Christian Church from the Apostles Times, as was done when the *Nicene Creed* was made; and a Faction in the Church assuming to it self the Title of *Catholick,* and proceeding by other rules, than the first Councils did, and imposing new Opinions and Practices, as things necessary to the Communion of the *Catholick Church.* And this is the true Point in difference between us, and those of the Roman Church about the *Churches Authority* in matters of Faith, since the *Council of Trent.* For we think we have very great reason to complain, when a Party in the Church, the most corrupt and obnoxious, takes upon it self to define many new Doctrines, as necessary Points of Faith, which have neither Scripture, nor Universal Tradition for them.

It

It were a very irrational thing, we are told, *to make Laws for a Countrey, and leave it to the Inhabitants to be Interpreters and Judges of those Laws; for then every Man will be his own Judge, and by consequence no such thing, as either Right or Wrong.*

But is it not as *irrational* to allow an *Usurper* to interpret the *Laws* to his own advantage, against the just Title of the Prince, and the true Interest of the People ? And if it be not Reasonable for any private Person to be *his own Judg,* why should a publick Invader be so ? But we hope it will be allowed to the Loyal Inhabitants of a Country, so far *to interpret the Laws,* as to be able to understand the Duty they owe to their King, and to justifie his Right against all the Pretences of Usurpers. And this is as much as we plead for in this case.

Can we therefore suppose, That God Almighty would leave us at those uncertainties, as to give us a Rule to go by, and leave every Man to be his own Judge ?

And can we reasonably suppose, *That God Almighty should give us a Rule* not capable of being understood by those *to whom it was given,* in order to the great End of it, *viz.* the saving of their Souls ? For this was the main end of the Rule, to direct us in the way to Heaven, and not meerly to determine Controversies. The Staff, which a Man uses, may serve to measure things by, but the principal design is to walk with it. So it is with the Holy Scripture, if Controversies arise : It is fit to examine and compare them with this Infallible Rule ; but when that is done, to help us in our way to Heaven is that which it was chiefly intended for. And no Man can think it of equal consequence to him; not to be mistaken, and not to be damned. In matters of Good and Evil, every mans Conscience is his immediate judge, and why not in matters of Truth and Falshood ? Unless we suppose mens involuntary mistakes to be more dangerous than their wilful sins.

But after all, *We do not leave every Man to be his own Judge,* any further than it concerns his own Salvation, which depends upon his particular Care and Sincerity. For to prevent any dangerous Mistakes by the Artifice of Seducers, we do allow the Assistance of those Spiritual Guides, which God hath appointed in his Church, for the better instructing and governing private Persons : We embrace the Ancient Creeds, as a summary comprehension of the Articles of Faith ; and think no Man ought to follow his own particular Fancy against Doctrines so universally received in the Christian Church, from the Apostles Times.

B

I do

I do ask any Ingenuous Man, whether it be not the same thing to follow our own Fancy, or to interpret Scripture by it.

If we allowed no Creeds, no Fathers, no Councils, there might have been some colour for such a Question. But do we permit Men to interpret Scripture according to their own Fancy, who live in a Church, which owns the Doctrine of the Primitive Church more frankly and ingenuously, than any Church in the World besides, without setting up any private Spirit against it, or the present *Roman Church* to be the Interpreter of it. And now I hope I may have leave to ask some Questions of any ingenuous Man; as, whether it be not the same thing for the Church of *Rome* to make the Rule, as to assume to it self the sole Power of giving the sense of it? For what can a Rule signify without the sense? And if this were the intention of Almighty God, had it not been as necessary to have told us, to whom he had given the Power of Interpreting the Rule, as to have given the Rule it self? Whether it be reasonable for the Church of *Rome,* to interpret those Texts, wherein this Power of Interpreting, is to be contained? For this is to make it *Judge in its own Cause,* which was thought an Absurdity before. And whether it be not as mischievous to allow a Prosperous Usurper the Power of Interpreting Laws, according to his own Interest, as any private Person, according to his own Fancy? Whether it be possible to reform Disorders in the Church, when the Person principally accused is Supream Judge? Whether those can be indifferent Judges in Councils, who beforehand take an Oath, to defend that Authority which is to be Debated? Whether *Tradition* be not as uncertain a Rule, as Fancy, when Men judge of Tradition according to their Fancy?

I would have any Man shew me, where the Power of deciding matters of Faith is given to every particular Man.

If by *deciding Matters of Faith* be understood the determining them in such a manner, as to oblige others, I do not know where it is given to every particular Man, nor how it should be. For then *every particular Man* would have a Power over *every particular Man*; and there would want a new Decision, whose should take place. But if *by deciding Matters of Faith,* no more be meant, but every mans being satisfied of the Reasons, why he believes one thing to be true, and not another; that belongs to *every Man,* as he is bound to take care of his Soul, and must give an account here to God and Man of the Reason of his Faith. And what can be meant in Scripture by *Proving all things, and holding fast that which is good,* 1 Thess 5.21. By *trying the Spirits, whether they be of God,* 1 John 4.1.

By

By *judging of themselves what is right,* Luke 12. 57. unless God had given to Mankind a Faculty of discerning truth and falshood in Matters of Faith. But if every Man hath not such a Power, how comes he to be satisfied about the Churches Authority? Is not that a Matter of Faith? And where ever any Person will shew me, that every Man hath a Power to determine his Faith in that matter, I'le undertake to shew him the rest.

Christ left his Power to his Church, even to forgive Sins in Heaven, and left his Spirit with them, which they exercised after his Resurrection.

But where then was the *Roman Catholick Church?* And how can it be hence inferred, That these Powers are now in the Church of *Rome,* exclusive to all others, unless it be made appear that it was *Heir-General to all the Apostles?* I suppose it will be granted, that the Apostles had some gifts of the Spirit, which the Church of *Rome* will not in Modesty pretend to; such as the Gift of Tongues, the Spirit of Discerning, Prophesie, Miraculous Cures and Punishments. Now, here lies the difficulty, to shew what part of the Promise of the Infallible Spirit (for the ordinary *Power of the Keys* relates not to this matter) was to expire with the Apostles, and what was to be continued to the Church in all Ages. A Promise of Divine Assistance is denied by none but *Pelagians*: But how far that extends, is the Question. In the Souls of good Men it is so as to keep them in the way to Heaven, but not to prevent any lapse into sin; and it were worth our knowing, where God hath ever promised to keep any Men more from Error, than from Sin. Doth he hate one more than the other? Is one more disagreeing to the Christian Doctrine than the other? How came then so much to be said for the keeping Men from Error, when at the same time, they confess they may not only commit great sins, but err very dangerously in the most Solemn manner, in what relates to the Doctrine of Manners. Would any have believed the Apostles Infallible, if they had known them to be Persons of ill Lives; or that they had notoriously erred in some Rules of great Consequence to the Welfare of Mankind? Now, all this is freely yielded, as to the Pretence of Infallibility in the Church of *Rome.* It is granted, that the Guides of that Church have been very bad Men; and that in Councils they have frequently erred about the Deposing Power, being only a *Matter of Practice,* and not of Faith. Whether it be so or not, I now dispute not; but it is granted, that notwithstanding this Infallible Spirit, the *Roman Church* may grosly err in a matter of mighty Consequence to the Peace of Christendom; and yet it cannot err in decreeing the least Matters of Faith. As for Instance, it can by no means err about the *seven Sacraments,* or the *Intention of the Priest about them;* but it may err about *Deposing Princes,* and *Absolving Sub*

jects

jects from their *Allegiance*: Which in easier terms is, They can never err about their own Interest, but they may about any other whatsoever.

I pass over the next Paragraph, the sense being imperfect, and what is material about the Creeds, hath been spoken to already.

That which next deserves Consideration, is,

That the Church was the Judge even of the Scripture it self, many years after the Apostles, which Books were Canonical, and which were not.

We have a distinction among us of *Judges* of the *Law* and *Judges* of the *Fact*: The One declares what the *Law* is, the *Fact* being supposed; the Other gives judgment upon the *Fact*, as it appears before them. Now in this Case about the *Canonical Books,* the Church is not judge of the Law. For they are not to declare whether a Book appearing to be *Canonical* ought by it to be received for *Canonical*; (which is taken for granted among all Christians) but all they have to do, is to give judgment upon the Matter of Fact, *i. e.* whether it appear upon sufficient Evidence to have been a Book written by Divine Inspiration. And the *Church of Rome* hath no particular Priviledge in this matter, but gives its Judgment as other parts of the Christian World do: And if it takes upon it to judge contrary to the general sense of the Christian Church, we are not to be concluded by it; but an Appeal lyes to a greater Tribunal of the Universal Church.

And if they had this Power, then I desire to know, how they came to lose it ?

Who are meant by *They*? And what is understood by *this Power*? It is one thing for a Part of the Church to give Testimony to a matter of Fact, and another to assume the Power of making Books *Canonical*, which were not so. This latter no Church in the World hath, and therefore can never lose it: The former is only Matter of Testimony, and all parts of the Church are concerned in it, and it depends as other Matters of Fact do, on the Skill and Fidelity of the Reporters.

And by what Authority Men separate themselves from that Church ?

What Church? The Catholick and Apostolick? We own no Separation from that; but we are dis-joined from the Communion of the *Roman Church,* that we may keep up the stricter Union with the truly *Catholick* and *Apostolick* Church. And this is no *Separating our selves,* but being cast out by an Usurping Faction in

the

the Church; becauſe we would not ſubmit to the unreaſonable Conditions o Communion impoſed by it; the chief whereof is owning all the Uſurpation, which hath by degrees been brought into it. To make this plain by an Example : Suppoſe a proſperous Uſurper in this Kingdom had gained a conſiderable Intereſt in it, and challenged a Title to the whole, and therefore required of all the Kings Subjects, within his Power, to own him to be Rightful King : Upon this, many of them are forced to withdraw, becauſe they will not own his Title : Is this an act of *Rebellion,* and not rather of true Loyalty ? Schiſm in the Church is like Rebellion in the State. The Pope declares himſelf *Head* of the *Catholick Church,* and hath formed himſelf a kind of Spiritual Kirgdom in the Weſt ; although the other parts of the Chriſtian World declare againſt it, as an Uſurpation. However, he goes on, and makes the owning his Power a neceſſary Condition of being of his Communion. This many of the Weſtern Parts, as well as Eaſtern, diſown and reject, and therefore are excluded Communion with that Church, whereof he is owned to be the *Head.* The Queſtion now is, Who gives the Occaſion to this Separation ? whether the Pope, by requiring the owning his Uſurpation, or We, by declaring againſt it ? Now, if the Conditions, he requires, be unjuſt and unreaſonable ; if his Authority, he challenges, over the *Catholick Church,* be a meer Uſurpation (for which we have not only the Conſent of the other Parts of the Chriſtian World, but of Scripture and the Ancient Church) then we are not to be condemned, for ſuch a Separation, which was unavoidable, if we would not comply with the Pope's Uſurpation. And upon this Foot the Controverſie about Schiſm ſtands between Us and the Church of *Rome.*

The only Pretence I ever heard of, was, becauſe the Church hath fail'd in wreſting and interpreting the Scripture contrary to the true ſenſe and meaning of it ; and that they have impoſed Articles of Faith upon us, which are not to be warranted by Gods Word. I do deſire to know who is to be Jugde of that, whether the whole Church, the Succeſſion whereof hath continued to this day without interruption ; or particular Men, who have raiſed Schiſms for their own advantage.

The whole force of this Paragraph depends upon a Suppoſition, which is taken for granted, but will never be yielded by Us, and we are ſure can never be proved by thoſe of the *Church* of *Rome,* viz. That in the new impoſed Articles, the *whole Church* in a continued Succeſſion hath been of the ſame

judgment

judgment with them, and only some *few Particular Men* in thefe laſt Ages have oppoſed them. Whereas the great thing we inſiſt upon next to the Holy Scripture, is, that they can never prove the Points in difference, by an Univerſal Tradition from the Apoſtles Times, either as to the *Papal Supremacy*, or the other Articles defined by the *Council of Trent*. We do not take upon our ſelves to contradict the Univerſal ſenſe of the Chriſtian Church from the Apoſtles Times in any one Point. But the true Reaſon of the proceeding of the *Church* of *England* was this. While the Popes Authority was here received and obeyed, there was no liberty of ſearching into abuſes, or the ways of Reforming them. But when Men were encouraged to look into the Scripture, and Fathers, and Councils, they ſoon found the ſtate of things in the Church extreamly altered from what they ought to have been, or had been in the Primitive Church: But they ſaw no poſſibility of Redreſs, as long as the Popes Authority was ſo abſolute and inviolable. This therefore in the firſt place they ſet themſelves to the accurate Examination of, and the Reſult was, that they could find it neither in the Scriptures, nor Fathers, nor Councils, nor owned by the Eaſtern Churches: And therefore they concluded it ought to be laid aſide, as an Uſurpation. Our Church being by this means ſet free (even with the conſent of Thoſe, who joined with the Church of *Rome* in other things) a greater liberty was then uſed in examining particular Doctrines and Practices, which had crept into the Church by degrees, when Ignorance and Barbariſm prevail'd; and having finiſh'd this enquiry, Articles of Religion were drawn up, wherein the ſenſe of our Church was delivered, agreeable to Scripture and Antiquity, though different from the Modern Church of *Rome*; and theſe Articles are not the private ſenſe of particular Men, but the Publick Standard whereby the World may judge, what we believe and practiſe; and therefore theſe are the ſenſe of our Church, and not the opinions or fancies of particular Men. And thoſe who call the retrenching the Popes exorbitant Power by the name of Schiſm, muſt by parity of reaſon call the caſting off an Uſurper Rebellion. But certainly thoſe who conſider the mighty advantages and privledges of the *Clergy* in the *Church* of *Rome*, can never reaſonably ſuſpect any of that Order ſhould hope to better themſelves by the Reformation. And if we judge of Mens actings by their Intereſt, one of the moſt ſurpriſing conſiderations at this day is, that the *Clergy* ſhould be *againſt*, and *Princes* for the *Church* of *Rome*.

A N

AN
ANSWER
TO THE
SECOND PAPER.

*I*T is a sad thing to consider, what a world of Heresies are crept into this Nation.

But is it not a strange thing to consider, that no distinction is here put between the *Religion by Law established*, and the Parties disowned by it, and dissenting from it? And yet many of these, though justly liable to the charge of *Schism*, embrace no Heresies against the Four or Six first General Councils. But if the Dissenters were guilty of never so many Heresies, how comes the *Church* of *England* to bear the blame of them; when the weakning its Power and Authority was the occasion of such an overflowing of *Schisms* and *Heresies* among us? And it is indeed a sad thing to consider how many Ways and Means have been used by all Parties to introduce and keep up *Schisms* and *Divisions* amongst us, and then how the *Church* of *England* is blamed for not being able to suppress them. But if all Doctrines opposite to the *Church* of *Rome* be accounted *Heresies*, then we desire to be informed, how the *Church* of *Rome* came to have this Power of defining Heretical Doctrines; or how any Doctrine comes to be *Heresie* by being contrary to its definitions. For *Heresie is an obstinate opposing some necessary Article of Faith.* It must therefore be proved, that what the *Church* of *Rome* declares, doth thereby become a necessary Article of Faith, or it is very unreasonable to lay the imputation of *Heresie* upon us. And this can never be maintained, without proving that the *Church* of *Rome* hath a Power to make Doctrines not necessary before, to become necessary by her Definition: which is the same thing with making

New

New Articles of Faith. But thefe can never be proved to be fuch by Univerfal Tradition; which the *Church* of *Rome* pretends for all her Articles of Faith.

Every Man thinks himfelf as competent a Judge of Scripture, as the very Apoftles themfelves.

Doth *Every Man* among us pretend to an infallible Spirit? and yet *Every Man* owns that the Apoftles had it. But what is meant by *being a Judge of Scripture?* If no more be underftood, than that *every Man* muft ufe his underftanding about it, I hope this is no Crime nor *Herefie.* The Scripture muft be believed in order to Salvation, and therefore it muft be underftood; for how can a Man believe, what he underftands not the fenfe or meaning of? If he muft underftand the fenfe he muft be *Judge of the fenfe*; fo that every Man, who is bound to believe the Scripture in order to his Salvation, muft be Judge of the fenfe of the Scripture, fo far as concerns his Salvation. But if by being a *Judge of the Scripture* be meant giving fuch a judgment, as obliges others to fubmit to it, then among us no particular Man doth pretend to be a *competent Judge of Scripture*, fo as to bind others to rely upon his Authority in expounding Scripture. We own the Authority of Guides in the Church, and a due fubmiffion to them, but we do not allow them to be as *competent Judges of Scripture as the very Apoftles.*

And 'tis no wonder it fhould be fo, fince that part of the Nation, which looks moft like a Church, dares not bring the true Arguments againft the other Sects, for fear they fhould be turned againft themfelves, and confuted by their own Arguments.

This is directly level'd againft the *Church* of *England*, which is hereby charged with Infincerity or Weaknefs in dealing with the Diffenters. But we muft confider the meaning of this Charge, *It is no wonder it fhould be fo, i. e. That every Man fhould think himfelf as competent a Judge of Scripture, as the very Apoftles, becaufe the Church of England dares not ufe the true Arguments againft the Sects.* Whence it appears that this true Argument is the Churches *infallible Authority*, and the Obligation of all Members of the Church to fubmit their judgments intirely thereto. I confefs that if the *Church* of *England* did pretend to this againft the *Sectaries*, they might juftly turn it againft her; becaufe in our Articles, tho the *Churches Authority* be afferted, yet *Infallibility* is denyed. If there can be no Authority in a *Church*, without Infallibility; or there can be no obligation to fubmit to Authority, without it, then the *Church* of *England* doth not ufe the beft Arguments againft Sectaries. But if there be no ground for Infallibility, if the Church which hath moft pretended to it, hath been moſt groſly deceived, if the Heads of that Church have been not barely ſuſpected of *Hereſie*, but one of them ſtands condemned for it in Three General Councils, own'd by that Church; then for all that I can ſee, the *Church of England* hath wiſely diſowned the pretence of Infallibility, and made uſe of the beſt Arguments againſt Sectaries from a juſt Authority, and the ſinfulneſs and folly of the Sectaries refuſing to ſubmit to it.

The Church of England (as 'tis called) would fain have it thought, That they are Judges in matters Spiritual, yet dare not ſay poſitively, there is no Appeal from them.

Is not the *Church of England* really what it is called? I would fain know what it wants to make it as good a *Church*, as any in the Chriſtian World? It wants neither *Faith* (if the Creed contain it) nor *Sacraments*, (and thoſe entire) nor *Succeſſion of Biſhops*, (as certain as *Rome* it ſelf) nor a *Liturgy*, (more agreeing to Primitive Worſhip, than is any where elſe to be found.) Why then *the Church of England, as 'tis called?* Well! But what is this *Church* now blamed for: They pretend to be *Judges in matters Spiritual*, and yet dare not ſay there is no appeal from them. How then? Are there no true Judges, but ſuch as there lies no Appeal from? There lies an Appeal from any Judges in the Kings Courts to the Court of Parliament; are They not therefore true Judges in *Weſtminſter-Hall*? There lay an Appeal from Biſhops to Metropolitans, from them to Patriarchs, from Patriarchs to General Councils, according to the Antient Polity of the Church. Were there therefore no true Judges, but General Councils?

What follows relating to the *Churches Authority*, and *every Mans following his own judgment*, hath been anſwered already. I proceed therefore, to what further concerns this matter of Appeal.

What Countrey can ſubſiſt in Quiet, where there is not a Supream Judge, from whence there can be no Appeal?

The natural conſequence from hence appears to be, That every *National Church* ought to have the *Supream Power* within it ſelf. But how come Appeals to a foreign Juriſdiction to tend to the Peace and Quiet of a Church? They have been always complained of in the beſt Ages of the Church, and by the beſt Men; ſuch as St. *Cyprian* and St. *Auguſtine* and the whole *African Churches*. The worſt Men began them, and the worſt Church encouraged them, without regard to the Peace of the *Chriſtian Church*, ſo it increaſed its own Grandeur by them.

C

We

We have had these hundred Years past, the sad effects of denying to the Church, that Power in matters Spiritual, without an Appeal.

And our Anceſtors for many hundred Years laſt paſt, found the intolerable Inconveniencies of an Appeal to foreign Juriſdiction. Whereby the Nation was exhauſted, Juſtice obſtructed, the Clergy oppreſſed, and the Kings Prerogative greatly diminiſhed. *But theſe were ſlight things in Compariſon to what we have felt theſe hundred Years paſt for want of it.* Have not the Kings Courts been open for matters of Law and Juſtice, which have been fill'd with Men of as great Abilities and Integrity, ſince the Reformation as ever they were before? Hath not the Appeal to the King in his High Court of *Chancery* been as much for the King & People, as ever the Appeal was to the Court of *Rome?* Have not all the Neighbour Princes been forced for the preſerving their own Dignity to ſet Bounds and Limits to Appeals to *Rome,* and to Orders or *Bulls* that come from thence? How then comes the want of ſuch an Appeal to be thought to produce ſuch ſad effects here? All Chriſtendom groans under the ſad effects of them: and it is a very ſelf-denying humour for thoſe to be moſt ſenſible of the want of them, who would really ſuffer the moſt by them.

Can there be any Juſtice done, where the Offenders are their own Judges, and equal Interpreters of the Law, with thoſe that are appointed to Adminiſter Juſtice?

And is there any likelihood, Juſtice ſhould be better done in another Country, by another Authority, and proceeding by ſuch Rules, which in the laſt reſort, are but the Arbitrary will of a Stranger. And muſt ſuch a one, pretending to a Power he hath no right to, be *Judge in his own Cauſe,* when he is the greateſt offender himſelf? But how is this applied to the *Proteſtants* in *England?*

This is our Caſe, here in England, *in matters Spiritual; for the Proteſtants are not of the Church of* England, *as 'tis the true Church, from whence there can be no Appeal; but becauſe the Diſcipline of that Church is conformable at preſent to their fancies; which, as ſoon as it ſhall contradict or vary from, they are ready to embrace or join with the next Congregation of People, whoſe Diſcipline or Worſhip agrees with the Opinion of that Time.*

The ſenſe of this Period is not ſo clear, but that one may eaſily miſtake about it. That which is aimed at, is, that we of the *Church* of *England,* have no tie upon us,
                                                                                      but

but that of our own judgments; and when that changes, we may join with *Independents* or *Presbyterians*, as we do now with the *Church of England.* And what security can be greater, than that of our Judgments? If it be said *to be nothing, but fancy and no true Judgment*, we must beg leave to say, that we dare Appeal to the World, whether we have not made it appear, that it is not *Fancy*, but *Judgment* which hath made us firm to the *Church of England.* Might it not as well have been said, that *the Protestants* of the *Church of England, adhered to the Crown in the Times of Rebellion out of Fancy, and not out of Judgment? And that if their Fancy changed, they might as well have joined with the Rebels?* Will not this way of Reasoning hold as strongly against those of the *Church of Rome*? For why do any adhere to that, but because it is agreeable to their Judgment so to do? What evidence can they give, that it is *Judgment* in them, and only *Fancy* in us? If Reason must be that which puts the difference, we do not question, but to make ours appear to be *Judgment*, and theirs *Fancy*? For what is an *infallible Judge*, which Christ never appointed, but *Fancy*? What is their *unwritten Word*, as a Rule of Faith to be equally received with the Scriptures, but *Fancy*? What is giving honour to God by the *Worship of Images*, but *Fancy*? What is making *Mediators* of *Intercession*, besides the *Mediator of Redemption*, but *Fancy*? What is the Doctrine of *Concomitancy*, to make amends for half the Sacrament, but *Fancy*? What is the *substantial Change of the Elements into the Body of Christ*, but *Fancy*? for both Senses and Reason are against it. What is the *deliverance of Souls out of Purgatory, by Masses for the Dead*, but meer Fancy? But I forbear giving any more Instances.

So that according to this Doctrine, there is no other Church nor Interpreter of Scripture, but that which lies in every Man's giddy Brain.

Let *Mens Brains* be as *giddy*, as they are said to be, for all that I can see, they are the best faculties they can make use of, for the understanding of Scripture, or any thing else. And is there any Infallible *Church* upon Earth, which must not be beholding to Mens *giddy Brains* for believing it? And it may be, nevertheless *giddy* for doing it? For God sake why do any Men take the *Church* of Rome to be *Infallible*? Is it not, because their Understandings tell them they ought so to do? So that by this consequence, there is no *Infallible Church*, but *what lies in every Mans giddy Brain.*

I desire to know therefore of every serious Considerer of these things, whether the great Work of our Salvation ought to depend on such a Sandy Foundation as this?

I thank God I have seriously considered this matter, and must declare that I find no Christian Church built on a more *sandy Foundation*, than that, which pretends

to

to be setled *upon a Rock*; I mean, so far as it imposes the *new Faith of Trent*, as a neceſſary Condition of Salvation. Had we no other reaſon to embrace Chriſtianity, than such as they offer for theſe New Doctrines, I am much afraid Chriſtianity it ſelf, to all inquiſitive Men, would be thought to have but a *Sandy Foundation*. But what is this *Sandy Foundation* we build upon? Every Man's private judgment in Religion? No underſtanding Man builds upon his own Judgment, but no Man of underſtanding can believe without it. For I appeal to any *ingenious Man*, whether he doth not as much build upon his own Judgment, who chuſeth the *Church*, as he that chuſeth *Scripture* for his Rule? And he that chuſeth the *Church*, hath many more Dfficulties to conquer than the other hath. For the *Church* can never be a Rule without the *Scriptures*, but the *Scriptures* may without the *Church*. And it is no ſuch eaſy matter to find the *Churches Infallibility* in the *Scripture*. But ſuppoſe that be found, he hath yet a harder *Point* to get over, *viz.* How the Promiſes relating to the *Church* in general, came to be appropriated to the *Church of Rome*. Which a Man muſt have an admirable Faculty at diſcerning, who can find it out, either in Scripture, or the *Records* of the *Ancient Church*.

The places of Scripture which are brought about *Chriſt's being with his Church to the end of the World*, about *the Power to forgive Sins*; about the Clergy being *God's Labourers Husbandry, Building, having the Mind of Chriſt*; do as effectually prove *Infallibility* of the *Church of England*, as the *Church of Rome*; for I cannot diſcern the leaſt inclination in any of them to favour one againſt the other.

And pray conſider on the other ſide, that thoſe who reſiſt the Truth, and will not ſubmit to his Church, draw their Arguments from Implications, and far-fetch'd Interpretations, at the ſame time that they deny plain and poſitive Words : which is ſo great a Diſingenuity, that 'tis not almoſt to be thought that they can believe themſelves.

This is a very heavy Charge; To reſiſt the Truth, to deny plain and poſitive Words of Scripture ; to be guilty of great Diſingenuity, ſo as not to believe our ſelves, are faults of ſo high a nature, as muſt argue not only a bad Cauſe, but a very bad Mind. And *God forbid*, that thoſe of the *Church of England*, ſhould ever be found guilty of theſe things. But to come to Particulars ; Is it reſiſting *Truth*, or arguing from *Implications* and denying plain and poſitive Words of Scripture, to ſay, *We muſt not worſhip Images* ; *We muſt make God alone the Object of Holy Worſhip* ; We muſt give the Euchariſt in both kinds according to *Chriſt's expreß Inſtitution* ; We muſt underſtand our Prayers, when St. *Paul's* words are ſo clear about it: So far at leaſt we have *plain and poſitive Words of Scripture* on our ſide. And for *Implications*, and far-fetch'd *Interpretations* commend me to the *Pope's Bulls*, eſpecially when they have a mind to prove their Authority from Scripture ; which they can do from *In the beginning*, to the end of the *Apocalypse*. But that which feems to be aimed at here, is, *This is my Body*; wherein the words feem to be *plain and positive* on their fide, and our fenfe to be *from Implications, or far fetc'h Interpretations*. To which I Anfwer, That there are Expreffions in Scripture as *plain & positive* as this, which none think themfelves bound to underftand in their literal fenfe. For then we muft all believe, that God hath *Eyes* and *Ears*, a *Face*, *Hands* and *Feet*, as firmly, as that the Bread was then turned into Chrift's Body, when he fpake thofe words. And I would know, whether the Chriftian Church rejecting the Doctrine of Thofe *who made God to be like to Man*, was not chargeable with the fame *refifting the Truth, and denying plain & positive Words of Scripture*, as we are? And yet I hope the Chriftian *Church* did then believe it felf. Suppofe any fhould affert, *That the Rock in the Wildernefs, was really changed into Chrift's Body*; would not he have the very fame Things to fay againft thofe who denied it? For are not the Words *as plain and as positive, That Rock was Chrift?* But *Sacramental Expreffions*, by the confent of the *Chriftian Church*, and the very Nature of the Things, are of a different fenfe from *Logical Propositions*. And if this had been intended in the plain and literal fenfe, St. *Paul* would never have as plainly and positively called it *Bread* after Confecration; nor the *Cup* be faid to be the New Teftament in his Blood.

The Conclusion is:

Is there any other Foundation of the Proteftant Church, but that if the Civil Magiftrate pleafes, he may call fuch of the Clergy as he thinks fit for his turn at that time, and turn the Church either to Presbytery, or Independancy, or indeed what he pleafes? This was the way of our pretended Reformation here in England. *And by the fame Rule and Authority, it may be altered into as many Shapes and Forms as there are Fancies in Mens Heads.*

This looks like a very unkind Requital to the *Church* of *England*, for her Zeal in afferting the Magiftrate's Power againft a Foreign Jurifdiction; to infer from thence, that the Magiftrate may change the Religion here which way he pleafes. But altho we attribute the *Supream Jurifdiction* to the King; yet we do not queftion but there are *inviolable Rights of the Church*, which ought to be preferved againft the *Fancies* of fome, and the *Ufurpations* of others. We do by no means make our Religion mutable, according to the Magiftrate's pleafure. For the Rule of our Religion is unalterable, being the *Holy Scripture*; but the Exercife of it, is under the regulation of the Laws of the Land. And as we have caufe to be thankful to God, when *Kings are Nurfing Fathers to our Church*; fo we fhall never ceafe to pray for their continuing fo; and that in all things we may behave our felves towards them. as becomes *good Chriftians*, and *Loyal Subjects*

A N

AN
ANSWER
TO THE
THIRD PAPER.

THE Third Paper is said to be written by a Great Lady, *for the satisfa-*
ction of her Friends, as to the Reasons of *Her leaving the Communion of*
the Church of England, *and making her self a Member of the Roman*
Catholick Church. If she had written nothing concerning it, none
could have been a competent Judge of those Reasons or Motives she had for it,
but her self : but since she was pleased *to write this Paper to satisfy her Friends* ;
and it is thought fit to be publ'shed for general Satisfaction, all Readers have a
right to judge of the strength of them ; and those of the *Church of England,*
an Obligation to vindicate the Honour of it, so far as it may be thought to suffer
by them.

I am sensible how nice and tender a thing it is, to meddle in a Matter wherein
the Memory of so *Great a Lady* is so nearly concern'd ; and wherein such Circumstances are mentioned, which cannot fully be cleared, the Parties themselves
having been many Years dead : But I shall endeavour to keep within due bounds,
and consider this Paper with respect to the main Design of it, and take notice of
other Particulars so far as they are subservient to it.

The way of her *Satisfaction* must needs appear very extraordinary ; for towards the Conclusion she confesses, *She was not able, nor would she enter into*
Disputes with any Body. Now where the Difference between the two Churches
lies wholly in Matters of Dispute, how any one cou'd be truly satisfied, as to the
Grounds of leaving one Church, and going to the other, without entring into
matters of Dispute with any body, is hard to understand. If Persons be resolved
before-hand what to do, and therefore will hear nothing said against it, there is

no

no such way, as to declare they will *enter into no Dispute about it.* But what *Satisfaction* is to be had in this manner of proceeding? How could *one bred up in the Church of England, and so well instructed in the Doctrines of it,* ever satisfy her self in forsaking the Communion of it, without enquiring into, and comparing the Doctrines and Practices of both Churches? It is possible for Persons of Learning, who will take the pains of examining things themselves, to do that, without *entring into Disputes with any Body*; but this was not to be presumed of a Person of her Condition. For many things must fall in her way, which she could neither have the leisure to examine, nor the Capacity to judg of, without the Assistance of such who made it their business to search into them. Had she no Divines of the Church of *England* about her, to have proposed her Scruples to? None able and willing to give her their utmost Assistance in a Matter of such Importance, before she took up a Resolution of forsaking our Church? This cannot be imagined; considering not only her great Quality, but that just esteem they had for her whilst she continued so zealous and devout in the Communion of our Church.

But we have more than this to say. One of the Bishops who had nearest Relation to her for many Years, and who owns in Print, *That he bred her up in the Principles of the Church of* England, was both able and willing to have removed any Doubts and Scruples with respect to our Church, if she would have been pleased to have communicated them to him. And however she endeavoured to conceal her Scruples; he tells her, in his Letter to her (which he since printed for his own vindication) *That he had heard much Discourse concerning her wavering in Religion, and that he had acquainted her Highness with it, the Lent before the Date of this Paper*; and was so much concerned at it, that he obtained a Promise from her, *That if any Writing were put into her Hands by those of the Church of* Rome, *that she would send it either to him, or the then Bishop of* Oxford, whom he left in Attendance upon her. After which, he saith, *She was many Days with him at* Farnham; *in all which time she spake not one word to him of any Doubt she had about her Religion.* And yet this Paper bears Date, *Aug.* 20. that Year, wherein she declares her self changed in her Religion: So that it is evident she did not make use of the ordinary Means for her own Satisfaction, at least as to these Bishops who had known her longest.

But she saith, *That she spoke severally to two of the best Bishops we have in* England, *who both told her, there were many things in the Roman Church, which it were much to be wished we had kept; As Confession, which was no doubt commanded of God; that Pray-*

Preface to his Treatise. P. 5.

Letter to her Royal Highness from the Bp. of Winton. P. 3, 4.

Blandford.

Pag 14.

Sheldon *A. B.* of Canterb. Blanford *Bp.* of Worcester.

ing for the Dead, was one of the Ancient Things in Christianity; that for their parts they did it daily, though they would not own it.   And afterwards, pressing one of them very much upon the other Points; he told her, That if he had been bred a Catholick, he would not change his Religion; but that being of another Church, wherein he was sure were all things necessary to Salvation, he thought it very ill to give that Scandal, as to leave that Church wherein he received his Baptism.   Which Discourses, she said, did but add more to the desire she had to be a Catholick.

Blandford
Bishop of
Worcester.

This, I confess, seems to be to the purpose; if there were not some Circumstances and Expressions very much mistaken in the Representation of it: But yet suppose the utmost to be allow'd, there could be no Argument from hence drawn for leaving the Communion of our Church, if this Bishop's Authority or Example did signify any thing with her.   For supposing he did say, *That if he had been bred in the Communion of the Church of* Rome, *he would not change his Religion:* Yet he added, *That being of another Church, wherein were all things necessary to Salvation, he thought it very ill to give that Scandal, as to leave that Church wherein he had received his Baptism.* Now why should not the last words have greater force to have kept her in the Communion of our Church, than the former to have drawn her from it? For why should any Person forsake the Communion of our Church, unless it appears necessary to Salvation so to do? And yet this yielding Bishop did affirm, *that all things necessary to Salvation were certainly in our Church; and that it was an ill thing to leave it.* How could this add to her *desire of leaving our Church?* unless there were some other Motive to draw her thither, and then such small Inducements would serve to inflame such a Desire. But it is evident from her own words afterwards, that these Concessions of the Bishop could have no Influence upon her: for she declares, *and calls* God *to witness, that she would never have changed her Religion, if she had thought it possible to save her Soul otherwise.* Now what could the Bishop's words signify towards her Turning, when he declares just contrary, viz. not only that it was possible for her to be saved without turning, *but that he was sure we had all things necessary to Salvation; and that it was a very ill thing to leave our Church?* There must therefore have been some more secret Reason, which *encreased her Desire to be a Catholick after these Discourses:* unless the Advantage were taken from the Bishop's calling the *Church of* Rome *the Catholick Religion; If he had been bred a Catholick, he would not have chang'd his Religion.* But if we take these words so strictly, he must have contradicted himself; for how could he *be sure we had all things necessary to Salvation,* if we were out of the Catholick Church? Was a Bishop of our Church, and one of the best Bishops of our Church, as she said, so weak as to yield, *That he was sure all things necessary to Salvation were to be had out of the Communion of the Catholick Church?*

But

But again; there is an inconfiftency in his faying, *That he thought it very ill to leave our Church*; which no Man of common fenfe would have faid, if he had believed the *Roman Church* to be the *Catholick*, exclufive of all others that do not join in Communion with it.

The utmoft then that can be made of all this, is, That there was a certain Bifhop of this *Church*, who held *both Churches* to be fo far *Parts of the Catholick Church*, that there was no neceffity of going from one *Church* to another. But if he afferted that, he muft overthrow the *neceffity* of the *Reformation*, and confequently not believe our *Articles* and *Homilies*, and fo could not be any true Member of the *Church* of *England*.

But the late Bifhop of *Winchefter* hath made a fhorter Anfwer to all th's; For he firft doubts, *Whether there ever were any fuch Bifhops who made fuch Anfwers;* And afterwards he affirms, *That he believes there never was, in Rerum Naturâ, fuch a Difcourfe as is pretended to have been between this Great Perfon, and two of the moft Learned Bifhops of* England. But, God be thanked, the Caufe of our Church doth not depend upon the fingular Opinion of one or two Bifhops in it, wherein they apparently recede from the eftablifh'd Doctrine of it. And I am fure thofe of the *Church* of *Rome* take it ill from us, to be charged with the Opinion of Particular Divines, againft the known Sentiments of their Church. Therefore fuppofing the Matter of Fact true, it ought not to have moved her to any Inclination to leave the *Church* of *England*.

Preface, p. 2.
p. 4.

But after all, *She protefts, in the Prefence of Almighty God, that no Perfon, Man or Woman, directly or indirectly, ever faid any thing to her (fince fhe came into* England*) or ufed the leaft Endeavour to make her change her Religion; and that it is a Bleffing fhe wholly owes to Almighty God.* So that the Bifhops are acquitted from having any hand in it, by her own words; and as far as we can underftand her meaning, fhe thought her felf converted by immediate Divine Illumination. We had thought the pretence to a *private Spirit* had not been at this time allowed in the *Church* of *Rome.* But I obferve, that many things are allowed to bring Perfons to the *Church* of *Rome*, which they will not permit in thofe who go from it. As the ufe of Reafon in the Choice of a Church; the Judgment of Senfe; and here, that which they would feverely condemn in others as a Private Spirit, or *Enthufiafm*, will pafs well enough if it doth but lead one to their Communion. Any Motive or Method is good enough which tends to that end; and none can be fufficient againft it. But why may not others fet up for the Change as to other Opinions upon the fame Grounds, as well as this Great Perfon does, as to the Change from our *Church* to the *Church* of *Rome?* And we have no Pretenders to *Enthufiafm* among us, but do as folemnly afcribe *the Bleffing wholly to Almighty God*; and look on it as the Effect of fuch *Prayers* as fhe made to him in *France* and *Flanders*.

D

But

But I wonder a Person, who owed her Change so wholly to Almighty God, should need the Direction of an Infallible Church; since the utmost they can pretend to, is no more than to have such an Immediate Conduct; and the least that can be meant by it, is, that she had no Assistance from any other Persons. Which may not exclude her own *Endeavours*: but supposing them to be employed, and an Account to be here given of them: yet there is no Connexion between any of the *Premises*, and the *Conclusion* she drew from them; and therefore it must be Immediate Impulse, or some concealed Motive which determin'd her Choice.

The *Conclusion* was, That *she would never have changed, if she could have saved her Soul otherwise*. If this were true, she had good Reason for her Change; if it were not true, she had none; as it is most certain it was not. Now let us examine how she came to this *Conclusion*; and I will suppose it to have been just in the Method she sets it down in.

First, she faith, *She never had any Scruples till the* November *before; and then they began upon reading Dr.* Heylin's *History of the Reformation; which was commended to her as a Book to settle her; and there she found such abominable Sacriledg upon* Henry *the 8th's Divorce, King* Edward's *Minority, and Queen* Elizabeth's *Succession, that she could not believe the Holy Ghost could ever be in such Counsels*.

This was none of the best Advices given to such a Person, to read Dr. *Heylin*'s History for her Satisfaction. For there are two distinct Parts in the *History* of our *Reformation*: the one *Ecclesiastical*, the other *Political*: the former was built on Scripture and Antiquity, and the Rights of particular Churches; the other on such Maxims which are common to States-men at all Times, and in all Churches, who labour to turn all Revolutions and Changes to their own Advantage. And it is strange to me that a Person of so great Understanding should not distinguish these two. *Whether* Henry *the 8th were a good Man or not*; *Whether the Duke of* Somerset *raised his Estate out of the Church Lands*, doth not concern our present Enquiry; which is, Whether there was not sufficient Cause for a Reformation in the Church? And it there was. Whether our Church had not sufficient Authority to reform it self? And if so, Whether the Proceedings of our Reformation were not Justifiable by the Rules of Scripture and the Ancient Church? These were the proper Points for her to have considered, and not the particular Faults of Princes, or the Miscarriages of Ministers of State. Were not the Vices of *Alexander* the 6th and many other Heads of the *Church of* Rome for a whole Age together, by the Confession of their own greatest Writers, as great at least as those of H*enry* the 8th? And were these not thought sufficient to keep her from the *Church of* Rome; and yet the others were sufficient to make her think of leaving our *Church*? But Henry *the 8th's Church* was in Truth the *Church of* Rome under a *Political Head*, much as the *Church of Sicily* is under the King of Spain. All the difference is, Henry

the

the 8*th* took it as his own Right; the *King of Spain* pretends to have it from the Pope, by such Concessions, which the Popes deny. And suppose the King of *Spain's* Pretence were unlawful to that Jurisdiction which he challengeth in the Kingdom of *Sicily*; were this a sufficient Ground to justify the thoughts of Separation from the *Church* of *Rome*?

But the *Duke of* Somerset *raised his Estate out of Church-Lands, and so did many Courtiers in the Reign of Queen* El*z*abeth.

Are there not Miscarriages of the like nature in the *Church* of *Rome*? What is the *Popes making great Estates out of the Church-Lands*, for their Nephews to be Princes and Dukes? a thing not unheard of in our Age. And is it not so much worse to be done by the Head of the Church?

These she confesses *were* but *Scruples*; but such as occasioned *her examining the Points in difference by the Holy Scripture.* Now she was in the right way for Satisfaction, provided she made use of the best Helps and Means for understanding it; *and took in the Assistance of her Spiritual Guides.* But it seems, contrary to the Doctrine of the Church of *Rome* she found some things so easy there, that she *wondred she had been so long without finding them out.* And what were these? No less than *the Real Presence in the blessed Sacrament; the Infallibility of the Church, Confession, and Praying for the Dead.*

These were great Discoveries to be made *so easily*, considering how those of the *Church of Rome*, who have been most vers'd in these Matters, have found it so difficult to make them out from thence.

(1.) As to the *Real Presence*; as it is in the Dispute between us and the *Church of Rome*, it implies the Real and Substantial Change of the Elements into the Body and Blood of Christ. But where do our Saviour's words, in *calling the Sacrament his Body and Blood*, imply any such thing? The wisest Persons of the *Church of Rome* have confessed, that the bare words of our Saviour can never prove it; but there needs the Authority of the Church to interpret them in that sense. How then could she so easily find out that, which their most Learned Men could not? But there is nothing goes so far in such Discoveries as a willing Mind.

(2.) As to *Confession*. No doubt the Word is often used in Scripture, and therefore *easily found.* But the Question between us, is not about the Usefulness or Advantage of *Confession* in particular Cases, but the Necessity of it in all Cases, in order to Remission of Sins. And I can hardly believe any Bishop of our Church would ever say to her, *that Confession in this sense was ever commanded by God.* For then he must be damned himself if he did not confess every known Sin to a Priest. But some general Expressions might be used, that Confession of Sin was commanded by God; *Confess your Sins one to another*: But here is nothing of a particular Confession to a Priest, necessary in order to Forgiveness of Sin.

(3) As

(3.) As to *praying for the Dead;* It is hard to find any place of Scripture which seems to have any tendency that way, unless it be with respect to the *Day of Judgment,* and that very doubtfully. But how came this Great Person to think it not possible to be saved in our *Church,* unless we prayed for the Dead? How did this come to be a Point of Salvation? And for the *Practice* of it, she saith, *the Bishops told her they did it daily.* Whether they did it or not, or in what sense they did it, we cannot now be better informed: But we are sure this could be no Argument for her to leave the Communion of our Church, because she was told by these Bishops they did it, and continued in the Communion of it.

(4.) Lastly; As to *the Infallibility of the Church.* If this, as applied to the *Roman Church,* could be any where found in Scripture, we should then indeed be to blame not to submit to all the Definitions of it. But where is this to be found? Yes, *Christ hath promised to be with his Church to the end of the World.* Not with his *Church,* but with his *Apostles:* And if it be restrained to them, then *the end of the World* is no more than *always.* But suppose it be understood of the Successors of the Apostles; were there none but at *Rome?* How comes this Promise to be limited to the Church of *Rome;* and the Bishops of *Antioch* and *Alexandria,* and all the other Eastern Churches (where the Bishops as certainly succeeded the Apostles, as at *Rome* it self) not to enjoy the equal Benefit of this Promise? But they who can find the *Infallibility of the Church of Rome* in Scripture, need not despair of finding whatever they have a Mind to there.

But from this Promise she concludes, *That our Saviour would not permit the Church to give the Laity the Communion in One kind, if it were not lawfull so to do.* Now in my Opinion, the Argument is stronger the other way; The Church of *Rome* forbids the doing of that, which Christ enjoyned; therefore it cannot be Infallible, since the Command of Christ is so much plainer than the Promise of Infallibility to the Church of *Rome,*

But, from all these things laid together, I can see no imaginable Reason of any force to conclude, that *she could not think it possible to save her Soul otherwise,* than by embracing the Communion of the Church of *Rome.* And the Publick will receive this Advantage by these Papers, that thereby it appears, how very little is to be said by Persons of the greatest Capacity, as well as Place, either against the Church of *England,* or for the Church of *Rome.*

F I N I S.

ERRATA.

Page 3. line 10. for *siking,* read *sinking.*

Books Printed for and Sold by *Robert Thornton*, Bookseller, at the Sign of the Leather-Bottle, in *Skinner-Row*.

COpies of Two Papers written by the Late King *Charles* the Second of Bleſſed Memory, and Publiſhed by Command of his preſent Majeſty.---- Together with an Anſwer to the ſaid Papers.

An Abridgment of the Engliſh Military Diſcipline, Printed by His preſent Majeſties Eſpecial Command for the uſe of the Forces throughout His Dominions.

A Papiſt Miſrepreſented and Repreſented : or, a twofold Character of Popery. The one Containing a Sum of the Superſtitions, Idolatries, Cruelties, Treacheries, and wicked Principles of that Popery which hath diſturb'd this Nation above an hundred and fifty Years; fill'd it with Fears and Jealouſies, and deſerves the Hatred of all good Chriſtians. The other laying open that Popery which the Papiſts own and profeſs; with the chief Articles of their Faith, and ſome of the Principal Grounds and Reaſons, which hold them in that Religion. By *J. L.* one of the *Church* of *Rome.* To which is added, A Book Entituled, The Doctrines and Practices of the Church of *Rome*, truly Repreſented : In Anſwer to the aforeſaid Book. By a *Proteſtant* of the *Church* of *England.*

An Antidote againſt Popery, Shewing how a devout Soul in the midſt of the manifold diſtractions and diviſions about Religion, and Pretenſions, and Claims to the Church, may, againſt all Scruples, reſt ſatisfied, and ſetled in mind, and chearfully go on in Gods Service, to Salvation. By a Reverend Divine of the *Church* of *England.*

Officium Eubhariſticum, or a Preparatory Service to a devout and worthy Reception of the Lords Supper; to which is added a Meditation for every day in the Week.

The Fundamentals of the Proteſtant Religion aſſerted by Reaſon, as well as Scripture , written in French, by the Famous Monſieur *de Gombaud*; and Tranſlated into Engliſh by *Sidney Lodge*, &c.

Di-

(3.) As to *praying for the Dead*; It is hard to find any place of Scripture which seems to have any tendency that way, unless it be with respect to the *Day of Judgment*, and that very doubtfully. But how came this Great Person to think it not possible to be saved in our *Church*, unless we prayed for the Dead? How did this come to be a Point of Salvation? And for the *Practice* of it, She saith, *the Bishops told her they did it daily.* Whether they did it or not, or in what sense they did it, we cannot now be better informed. But we are sure this could be no Argument for her to leave the Communion of our Church, because she was told by these Bishops they did it, and continued in the Communion of it.

(4.) Lastly; As to the *Infallibility of the Church.* If this, as applied to the *Roman Church*, could be any where found in Scripture, we should then indeed be to blame not to submit to all the Definitions of it. But where is this to be found? Yes, *Christ hath promised to be with his Church to the end of the World.* Not with his *Church*, but with his *Apostles*: And if it be restrained to them, then the *end of the World* is no more than *always*. But suppose it be understood of the Successors of the Apostles; were there none but at *Rome*? How comes this Promise to be limited to the Church of *Rome*; and the Bishops of *Antioch* and *Alexandria*, and all the other Eastern Churches (where the Bishops as certainly succeeded the Apostles, as at *Rome* it self) not to enjoy the equal Benefit of this Promise? But they who can find the *Infallibility of the Church of Rome* in Scripture, need not despair of finding whatever they have a Mind to there.

But from this Promise she concludes, *That our Saviour would not permit the Church to give the Laity the Communion in One kind, if it were not lawfull so to do.* Now in my Opinion, the Argument is stronger the other way; The Church of *Rome* forbids the doing of that, which Christ enjoyned; therefore it cannot be Infallible, since the Command of Christ is so much plainer than the Promise of Infallibility to the Church of *Rome*.

But, from all these things laid together, I can see no imaginable Reason of any force to conclude, that *she could not think it possible to save her Soul otherwise,* than by embracing the Communion of the Church of *Rome*. And the Publick will receive this Advantage by these Papers, that thereby it appears, how very little is to be said by Persons of the greatest Capacity, as well as Place, either against the Church of *England*, or for the Church of *Rome*.

F I N I S.

ERRATA.

Page 3. line 10. for *fiking*, read *finking*.

CPSIA information can be obtained at www.ICGtesting.com

233483LV00003B/35/P